Don't just talk.

Do it

And make your crazy idea happen.

Nadine Horn

Don't just talk, Do it

Don't just talk, Do it!

By Nadine Horn

Copyright 2014 by Nadine Horn

Visit website: www.nadinehorn.com

Don't just talk, Do it

All rights are reserved: no part of this publication may be reproduced, stored in a retrieval system, or transmitted in any form by any means, electronic, mechanical, photocopying, recording, or otherwise without either the prior written permission of the author or a licence permitting restricted copying in the United Kingdom. This book may not be lent, resold, hired out or otherwise disposed of by way of trade in any form of binding or cover than in which way it is published, without the prior consent of the author.

Don't just talk, Do it

To mum and dad!
For never asking the question "why".

Für Mutti und Papa!
Dafür, dass sie keine zweifelnden Fragen
stellen, wenn ich mal wieder unterwegs bin.

Don't just talk, Do it

What is this book is about?

It's about doing and living it: your dream, your passion or your crazy idea. Realising that money is not always the most crucial thing and that you don't have to wait for the right moment to come – believe me it never does, you just have to get started. It's about taking a step now and start creating what you crave for.

In the book I show you in 7 steps how to create momentum to make your crazy idea happen: what tools matter and that worries, fears and doubts are normal once you encounter something new, but are no evidence of what is possible. I talk about stepping away of what you think you want and allow your idea to evolve naturally, to something more fun and bigger than you could have imagined at the start.

Let's take 30 days: What can happen in as little as a month? Daily catch-ups for morning coffees with

Don't just talk, Do it

your friends? Having repeated chats about **"what you would like to do, see or learn"**? Or preparing yourself to get ready for a sponsored cycle trip around whole Spain, learning Spanish on the way?

It took less time than this to set up my first real adventure: Mission Spain (www.nadinehorn.com -> Adventure -> Big). On the 1st April 2011 I had the crazy idea to cycle around Spain and get paid to be an adventurer. 30 days later I was sitting in a plane off to Madrid to pick up my sponsored bike. Two days after that I started my two-week language course, provided by LinguaSchools, to be ready for the real thing: cycling around Spain by myself, covering a challenging distance of over 4000km.

What took me 30 days to get off the ground – gave me a life intensive adventure for over two months in return: I washed myself in the blue river streams of green Asturias (north of Spain), cycled along vast fields of olive trees – and passed yellow oceans of orange scrubs

Don't just talk, Do it

releasing their fruity smell in the rising morning sunlight. I got my ripped bike trousers sewed up by a "bicigrino" (pilgrim on bike) from Iceland who cycled the medieval pilgrimage route the St. James Way (or in Spanish, Camino de Santiago de Compostela), drank cortados (espresso with milk – very popular in Spain) in a different village every day and had a motorist giving me company for two days, inviting me for typical meals along the way.

More than 5000 people followed my self-designed webpage, reading my posts (first appearing in English and later also in Spanish) and watching my videos – giving me company on my undertaking. After finishing my adventure, my story appeared in the German radio station 91.2 and in various newsletters. I was asked by one of my inspirational heroes John Williams (author of bestselling book "Screw Work Lets Play") to share my experience in front of his audience of his monthly meet-up event

Don't just talk, Do it

for creative people (www.scannercentral.co.uk).

This all was made possible by following some simple steps, asking for help when it was needed and not allowing bumps in the road to stop me. I use my journey to assist you with your own: sharing my bumps and what I did to keep moving, creating an incredible lifestyle and making a whole country my new home.

At the end you find a summary and some empty pages to make notes - use it.

Don't just talk, Do it

Don't just talk, Do it

A Story

I was staring at a picture hanging on the wall opposite to me – an artistically distorted version of a fictional coloured tree lined road. Everyday my eyes rested on the same strange (and boring) picture, every day I was looking at the same blue-grey painted wall – my office whose windows overlooking central London never changed, and I was wearing black – I was wearing corporate: black trousers, black high-heeled shoes (I found somewhere in my mums closet), everything within the acceptable frame of the corporate dress-code. My desk was clean, I could shift and shuffle the pen box or keyboard, but it did not make a difference. My in-tray was empty and the emails flowing into my inbox only came from people who were too lazy to edit and adjust the format of their documents and delegated the task to me. I hit the forward button and delegated them further.

Don't just talk, Do it

Everyday: Monday to Friday, the same surrounding,

the same people (with their same complaints) and the same uninspiring tasks. The only thing that reminded me of a bigger life-outside this room: a calendar picture behind me with a blue ocean and a sailing boat fighting its way through the waves. What a difference an adventure could make to my day?

You know this scenario? Good news, you can change it and escape your depressing office environment.

Don't just talk, Do it

Don't just talk, Do it

Doer vs. Talker

We can define people who just go out and do stuff as "doer" and those who only like to talk about things, but never take a step to make it happen, as "talker". There is nothing wrong with being a talker – assuming that you like to be one. If so, accept the fact and allow yourself to breathe, taking the guilt feeling off your shoulders that you haven't done anything yet and cancel the following out of your conversation with a "doer":

- I should do this

- I want to do this

- I have to do this

You are just giving yourself a hard time. If you secretly know that you never will move into the direction to do anything about it and agreed you are talker – let it go. Don't want to be one anymore?

Don't just talk, Do it

Like to step into the "doing loop" and become a "doer" – then keep reading: this book is going to help you with some inspiration, tools and good habits to turn you into one.

Are you a talker or a doer? Make the test

Not sure (or don't' want to admit) that you are a talker and not a "doer", well let's make the test. Read the sentences and then tick "yes" or "no", whatever seems to be more like you (yes you can do this in the book – it's yours). Do it now. (Next page)

Don't just talk, Do it

The Talker vs. Doer Quiz	Yes	No
Have you heard yourself saying over a year now that you like to learn this language?		
Are you jealous when your buddies are talking about their latest travel stories and you keep saying "I want to go there as well"?		
Do you catch up with your friends and keep complaining about things in your life rather than changing them?		
Do you wish your lifestyle to be different?		
Do you "do" a lot of things, but not producing the desired results, not getting anywhere?		

How many times have you ticked "yes"? More than you have ticked "no"? Well, then you are a talker (again, it's not a bad thing, it just is). You have two options now:

- Close the book and be a happy talker or

- Keep reading, transform into a doer and make your crazy ideas happen

If you have answered the last question with "yes",

Don't just talk, Do it

but most of the others with a "no" – first of all:

Congratulations !

You are a "doer" – you are just a bit "stuck", using up your energy in all kinds of directions, but on none in particular. Keep reading this book, it gives you some tools and insights to change this, helping you to evolve into a more efficient "doer" (this is what we all like).

Don't just talk, Do it

Table of Contents

Step One

    Just take your pick and get started   21

Step two

    Dare to dream big, yep, believe it's possible   53

Step three

    Let your project evolve naturally   75

Step four

    Ask for help   92

Don't just talk, Do it

Step five
 Dare to share – emotions, doubts and hey, your actual project 112

Step six

 Money is not the limiting factor to get you started 132

Step seven

 Done and dusted, enjoy the outcome 146

Don't just talk, Do it

Don't just talk, Do it

Just take your pick and get started

"The world is your playground. Why aren't you playing?"

-Ellie Katz, author, playologist and psychologist

This little chapter is actually a reminder to myself: just take your pick, stop worrying about where you are heading – and enjoy the moment of surprise. Don't think too much about the **"why you are doing it"** and **"the result"**, but choose one thing and have fun with it.

It is easier said than done and I tell you I had some troubles with it as well: At the beginning of 2011 I knew one thing: I was craving for something **"out in the wild"** and crazy like Indiana Jones searching for the "Holy Grail" – I was up for adventures and a change of lifestyle, but I had no idea where to start. I was in the **"I like to do this, but not actually doing it, loop"**, it's when you hear yourself talking

Don't just talk, Do it

about ideas and desires, but not taking a step towards making them happen - I was simply stuck, missing direction and had no inspiration in sight: Day in, day out sitting in a depressing office environment that was hit by the financial crisis with people slowly, but surely loosing their jobs.

The question at hand:

- How do you get out of this?

Adventures

A nice word to use if you are bored, depressed and lacking any kind of inspiration. The only thing I associated with the word at this point was **"Indiana Jones"** (how funny is that?), but I had no idea what it looked like in my own world.

Thinking more about it – trying to figure it out – did

Don't just talk, Do it

not help and I realized that in order to de-mystify the word adventure, I had to **"do"** things and find out. It was time to choose something, anything and take action.

Get moving, get unstuck

You are ready to change things, but don't know where to start? Well, here is something you can do that gets you directly on the moving track:

- Accept what is now, where you are and what you do

Let me explain with an example (remember school days?): Some time during my school years, I collected some pretty bad grades – nearly letting me fail to make it into the next year. Then there was a turning point, when all of a sudden things became

Don't just talk, Do it

easier, the struggle to sit down ceased and in the end I graduated as one of the top students of my year. What happened?

At one point, I realised that not-liking a particular subject didn't motivate me to spend any time on it, let alone grabbing good grades. I stopped fighting and accepted that in order to finish school, I had to pass it (nothing could change that). I concentrated on things I liked, creating fun **"ways of learning"**, such as using flashcards and setting myself the goal to memorise as much as possible, making some of the subject-content nearly irrelevant (such as history – sorry, wasn't my favourite). I saved my fighting-energy and used it for something that was moving me forwards. I looked at the elements I liked – or created them, moving away from **"wanting to change a fact, I couldn't",** in short: I got unstuck, I got moving.

Going back to your boring work- or unexciting

Don't just talk, Do it

lifestyle situation, the same principal applies here:

- Stop complaining and stop fighting what you cannot change right now, but look for the things that you enjoy – or the freedom it provides you to follow-up on some of your passions

Things are still going to change, but complaining does not get you anywhere (and only uses up your precious resources).

By the way, if it is work related, realise that **"you"** are not your work and that you are there by choice, not by force (the time of your mother's umbilical cord is long-time gone) – welcome the idea that it's not forever, but only until something-else hits your **"amazement button"** (and becoming a "doer" you will jump on it).

Don't just talk, Do it

No one traps you into something: the only trap is to wait until things change.

Even a 9-to-5 routine has advantages

...or:

"In the middle of difficulty lies opportunity"

-Albert Einstein

So I accepted the fact that I was stuck – in the good old 9-to-5 routine – that I wanted to change things, but was lacking the knowledge of what my desired lifestyle (the one as adventure) would resemble.

The next step was to look at the benefits of my situation instead of making it the foundation of complaints:

Don't just talk, Do it

- Weekends free
- Extra cash to spend
- 9-to-5: no work before, no work after
- Option to take leave: a day or two – even longer weekends

What I did was boring, but at the same time provided me with financial freedom and head-space (no thinking about work before 9am and no problem solving after 5pm). That was a start.

Next: What is it you don't like?

What do you want to have in your life (think work, think lifestyle)? A list of answers is popping up in your brain, ready to be spit out on paper? Great, if not don't panic, but ask yourself instead: What is it that you don't like, or even hate at the moment?

In my case, the first question left me confused with

Don't just talk, Do it

some blurred-sounding words (nothing concrete, cannot even remember), the second, however, gave me more to work with:

- Not learning anything that really mattered (and making a difference to my life outside work)

- No challenge in sight: neither physically (the walk to the kitchen, getting coffee and cookies or walking up the stairs instead of taking the lift does not count) nor mentally (Come on! Day in day out the same piles of papers)

- No positive surprises that extended my view on the world or life (people go to lunch when it's time not when they are hungry)

- The same faces (with their same ego-issues, complaints and outlook on life – and all about work)

Don't just talk, Do it

- Not surrounded by an visionary ideas that stimulated me to think bigger

- My energy worked for the business, not for myself (I did not get anything tangible to take home at the end of the day or created something that mattered to me)

Once I took the opposite of my list (you can do the same now for your list) – I knew what I was looking for:

- Learning something that matters and I can use outside work: something that expands my view or knowledge about life

- Stretch myself physically and mentally: do something I have not done before and learn things that matter along the way

- Be surprised by the day, rather than me planning what's going to happen (life is

Don't just talk, Do it

bigger than what we know)

- Get inspired by people

- Create something that matters to me and makes a difference in my life

It was all about: Experiencing life by living it outside the career and social template.

If you know what you like, you are ready for action and so was I: unplanned weekend trips to start ticking-off the **"I like to do this"** boxes, getting out of the talking loop and stepping into the doing one.

Forget the question **"If it is possible"** and make space for:

How to make it happen! (yeah baby)

Don't just talk, Do it

Too many options = too many questions = limbo

What a dilemma! (I am being funny here) Now you are ready to take-off, but have too many exciting things to choose from and don't know where to start? It's like the feeling that bubbles up inside of you when standing in front of a deliciously looking buffet and you don't have a clue what to eat first: you simply have too many options (and as a by-product you ask yourself too many questions). Let's check why we are giving ourselves such a hard time (and what we can do to sort ourselves out):

- It seems, your "gut-feeling" is sleeping and there is no instant impulse of "yeah, that's it"

- Now, if you decide without your intuition, you are afraid you select the wrong one (as I

Don't just talk, Do it

said: Dilemma!)

In my scenario, it was the question: where to go first on my weekend trips? There were so many places I liked to visit, but none of them swept me off my feet by the thought of it. Result: Limbo. I was ready to make a decision, but afraid that whatever I was going to choose, could not be the **"right"** one (alarm: old dusted thinking-pattern). Looking back now, it seems quiet easy what to do, however back then – it was a "problem" that emotionally tortured me. So what did I do?

Write it down

Sorting out the uncertainty in my head (where is the inspiration when you need it?), I decided that pen and paper were going to help me, or rather a word-document and my keyboard.

Once you start writing things down, you shift from being the victim, drowned by your thoughts, to

Don't just talk, Do it

being the observer – stepping away from the situation and looking at it from a different angle.

...but where, when and what to do? I had this situation where my mates tell me which trip they just booked and impressed me already with their latest travel stories to "wherever". I was honestly jealous. I know I like to travel, but simply had no clue where to start. So I thought right: Start somewhere and take your pick."

- post entry from Mission Spain

Writing this down, I became clear on the essence of what I associated with the word adventure:

- It was about exploring – going out and being

thrown into the unknown, meeting people and see what feelings are triggered by different locations

You can only experience **"what its like"** by going out and doing it. The post entry made me realise that a "wrong" option did not exist under this aspect and the problem of not choosing was simply an inner resistance with no foundation: It was time to trick it and take my pick.

Still not choosing, use of what's holding you back

If you cannot choose, ask yourself what was holding you back so far from doing it.

The questions I asked myself:

- What stopped me from hitting the "book"-button and visiting the places **"I wanted to go"**?

Don't just talk, Do it

The answer: money. For some reason, for the sake of an old-thinking pattern, I thought that I required a stack of cash to hit the road: first money, then the freedom to travel (sounds familiar?).

It was time to confront this belief and let **"the least amount of money"** choose where I was going: I travelled by the idea **"explore by price"** and book whatever was the cheapest and available: bus or planes and whatever location it was taking me (already sounded adventurous).

Change your direction as you go along

There is no perfect choice: Whatever you have selected, it is not going to last for eternity (and dooming you in hell). You decide how long you are going to have fun with it. Realise that you can always change and adjust the direction of what you are doing – believe me it's much more fun to get started and take off the pressure instead of wanting

Don't just talk, Do it

to achieve a "perfect" outcome in the first place.

I followed my own advice and dropped the expectation of creating a supreme adventure, but to go out and explore, filling the missing gaps as I went.

Accept your nature

One thing I know about myself is that I am not a good tourist, I am an anti-tourist: I don't visit museums for the sake of **"having been there"** or tick-off the "must-seen" list in a sightseeing-guide (I actually never bought one). For me it's all about discovering the city on my own terms and best of all with some physical edge, such as running a marathon in Barcelona and being overwhelmingly surprised to see the Gaudi Cathedral for the first time, or getting lost in New York, walking around for the whole day

Don't just talk, Do it

without having a map.

My motto:

- I will see what I am going to do, once I get there

And with the same approach I went on my first trips.

#1 Edinburgh: Unplanned walk with only one destination – hills

From London to Edinburgh with Megabus for only £10 return (three pints, or one weekend trip – that is what I call a bargain). I visited Edinburgh once, including the mouth dropping gigantous highlands with their rich green valleys. I always wanted to go back and see hills, so I did. Hopping of the bus in the centre of the medieval city – my rucksack strapped on my bag - visiting the highlands was out

Don't just talk, Do it

of question: too expensive to join an organised trip. I travelled with spending the least amount of money. So I started walking out of the urban part and discovered some mountains, emerging at the horizon (what a coincidence, but true).

As I had neither a schedule nor a plan, I decided to keep walking until I reached them (I know crazy, but hey, adventurous). Once I got there (and after a couple of hours I did), the hills only were the beginning of a stunning mountain range with old stone hedges, keeping the grazing sheep in place and a lake hiding in a lush valley - next to it, an old village with some orange cattle looking at me with desinterest once I passed - chewing on their hay.

What I liked about the trip:

- The timeless-ness of not having a fixed

Don't just talk, Do it

schedule (going where the wind blew me, soaking up the moment)

- Walking a long distance and satisfying the wish to see hills (one item crossed off my **"want to do"** list)

- The discovery of some beautiful spots, I could not have planned to see (Scottish cattle, never seen anything like this and would have not gone into the zoo to do so)

What I didn't like:

- The time was too short (well, weekend-trips)

- Did not plan where to sleep (saving money, you know)

- Physical challenge not challenging enough

Inspiration:

Don't just talk, Do it

- Sleeping in the wild

Norway: Discovering "Couchsurfing"

There were three points I did not like about my last trip - for the next one I said "good-bye" to one:

- No place to sleep

You can always "pay" for things, the point is to find ways to work around "money" and make it less important (and hence less limiting). All I really needed was a warm corner where I could have a nap for a couple of hours (instead of falling asleep in a pub and get kicked out) – nothing fancy.

I came across "Couchsurfing", an online-platform that connects people all over the world: if you have a spare sofa (or as a traveller, looking for one), you create a profile on the site and either make your

Don't just talk, Do it

couch "available" or "request" one - pretty handy when passing through towns for a short period of time.

The night before I boarded my plane (just found out about it last-minute), I signed up and sent a "Couch Request" to 10 people living around the area, I was about to visit. The next morning, checking my emails 10 minutes before I left the house, there was one reply – and hence one sofa.

Did I have any scary scenarios running through my head by the idea of sleeping on a strangers couch? Like:

- Walking into a filthy house with 17 cats or

- The door opened by a nudist-couple or

- Napping on the couch of a serial killer? (it's scary, but it can actually be a normal thought)

Don't just talk, Do it

Actually no, I chose the people after their profile picture and trusted my instincts. And hey, I told myself that once I knocked on the door and something set of my alarm bells – I could leave (with any blame excuse).

Trying out something new, you just have to trust yourself that you are going to be OK.

Cancelling out one dislike, the rest went without plan to keep the adventure spirit: landing at the snow covered airport in a country I had never been (wow - another item ticked off the **"haven't done**

Don't just talk, Do it

yet" list).

And I already had a mission: to find the house of my "Couchsurfing" host. As I had time until conquering my sofa, I decided to walk and somehow get there. I cuddled myself into my thick jacket and stepped through the snow – rising up to my calves - enjoying its crunching sound (this by itself was worth-while the trip). I walked and walked and walked: along empty streets with pine-tree forest lining up at the horizon and little Norwegian neighbourhoods – everything captured my interest, everything was new.

To make sure I was on the right track I entered a petrol station that I passed on the way, asking for direction. Not only was it the first time I chatted to some local, but at the same occasion discovered Norwegian food and sweets displayed at the counter (if you go where you have never been – everything is a new discovery that you normally

Don't just talk, Do it

take for granted in your home-town).

It's the surprise of the moment that blew my mind: like my host – a total stranger – caring about me throughout the day, texting once in a while to see if I was OK. Or his car completely buried under snow, parked in front of his place that stunned me once I reached my destination.

I knocked on the door and was welcomed with a big smile, an offer for a hot cup of tea and the words: make yourself at home. Within seconds the "stranger" was a friend and we chatted away like this. There was another "Couchsurfer" – a polish guy who just finished walking the St. James Way (still tanned from his Spain journey), now settling in Norway to learn the language and find some work in a ski resort. My host himself just came back from his 6-month cycle trip around Vietnam. I was inspired and my brain was soaking in the experience, making new connections for creating my own. I felt alive being surrounded by people

Don't just talk, Do it

with visions and creative ideas to brush up their skills – and most of all made friends in an instance skipping any non-sense talk. We connected because we had something in common: the curiosity about life and adventures.

I slept well, using my next day for a long walk: passing birch woodland and discovering a large water basin with massive chunks of broken ice layer, floating on top.

One weekend, one hell of a good experience

What I liked about the trip:

- To be inspired by fellow-explorers (as crazy and nutty as myself)

- Be part of the culture by having a home (and

Don't just talk, Do it

- watching Norwegian television)

- Trusting my instincts and making friends in an instance (cutting through "shit"-chat and getting to know each other straight away by being up-front and honest)

- Discovery of "Couchsurfing" (and the trust in strangers)

- Exploring Norwegians beautiful winter landscape

What was missing?

- Some physical endurance

Inspiration:

- Learning a new language by living in a different country (and becoming a child again, discovering the sounds and names of things like spoon, knife and fork)

Don't just talk, Do it

- Doing some crazy stuff, like walking the St. James Way or cycling around Vietnam

----

Germany: The first cycle adventure

Without even realising, every trip left behind a new idea or inspiration (at times subtle), plus created a new momentum, such as this one: Once I finished off my – finding the hills in – Scotland adventure and – meeting "fellow-nutties" in – Norway trip, I bumped into a friend. We started chatting, the usual update with a conversation similar to this:

- **Me:** What's new?

- **Him:** Nothing, work, work and work – you know. How about you?

- **Me:** Well, there was … (and the stories followed: a bombardment of exciting

Don't just talk, Do it

discoveries and adventures that happened in as less than two weekends)

His eyes brightened up and by the end of the chat, I made a promise: to involve him with my next journey. It only took me a couple of weeks until I dialled his number, asking if he would be keen to join a cycle trip in Germany. He was "in" and once we booked the flights, we sat down at my kitchen table, with a glass of wine (or rather a bottle) and planned our itinerary. The idea was to hire bikes at Lake Konstanz, pop over to the Black Forest and end the adventure in Zurich. This trip was going to cancel out the last **"what is missing"** bits:

- Lack of physical endurance (we were going to cover quiet a bit in 3 days)

- Time to short (I made use of my annual leave – taking two additional days off)

Even though we had a plan, we were flexible: when

Don't just talk, Do it

picking up our bikes at Lake Konstanz, we asked the owner – a local of the area – what he thought about our itinerary. He recommended cutting out the Black Forest for now and shortening it down to: Lake Konstanz to Zurich. So we did – still having many kilometres to kill (physical challenge here we come). Stuffing our two rear panniers (the bags you can hook on the back of your bike) with our tent, two sleeping bags and clothes, we hit the road. It was awesome and a real adventure: we cycled through the rain alongside Lake Konstanz – the third largest lake in Europe, slept outside behind some farm shed in Switzerland and tasted local beers in some old German villages where we stopped for a break (and a chance to dry our clothes). It was impressing, an adventure with pleasure, surprise, a purpose (arriving in Zurich) and a challenge: it was a complete success.

Don't just talk, Do it

What I liked about the trip:

- Everything, most of all the magical moments: cycling in the morning sunlight along frost covered fields, buying fresh milk from a Swiss farm or crawling out of the tent and being greeted by the stunning view of the alps, proudly presenting themselves on the other side of the lake

- The learning curve: we had no burner to cook our food on or warm-up ourselves (it was freaking cold) – couldn't make a fire because everything was moist (including the matches) and had problems setting up the tent

Inspiration:

- This adventure had everything. I realised that doing a longer trip of this kind would teach me a lot: solving problems as they

Don't just talk, Do it

occurred – I was hooked for more.

You see, I became clear on what I was after by doing things, slowly adjusting the dislikes until they were cancelled out. And not only this, every trip set ground for new inspirations.

Don't just talk, Do it

Don't just talk, Do it

Dare to dream big, yep, believe it's possible

After the taste of doing my little weekend adventures, I was ready to dream bigger.

We watch movies, fantasize and wish the character would be us: we dream like kids, but believe it's meant to stick around in fairy-tale land. Why not dreaming with the intention of making those ideas real? Believing that it is possible?

My dream:

- To be an adventurer

The bigger version:

- To actually get paid for it

Don't just talk, Do it

The outcome:

- Cycling around Spain with sponsored equipment, a bike and a language course. Cool hey?

What is big anyway?

To let go of being intimated by the word **"big"**, it's time to have a look at it: We like the word "big" because we think only if it is "big" enough, is it going to make a difference in our lives, right? So I thought. This belief only made things difficult for me: I was tuned into making my dream come true and - lucky me - came across a 30 Day Challenge where people committed themselves to do so. I signed up with the idea to get myself **"branded as adventurer"** (getting paid to be one).

Don't just talk, Do it

The next thing was to choose a venture – and that was the moment where "big" caused troubles: to get paid for what you love doing, get people being interested in what you do – I thought that I had to do something big. I tried to figure out this **"bigness"** with the following pattern as result:

- Doing a) would lead to b) and then to c) – by the time c) was reached, the idea was abandoned – it wasn't big enough

Every idea for an adventure that popped into my head was drowned by the above pattern. I didn't give it a chance to evolve and let it take shape outside my head. That's when I realised something:

- Big is not what people say it is, but what you make it to be

I only had 30 days to share something tangible in the **"30 Day Challenge Community"**. Following this logical, but not very helpful chase of **"big**

Don't just talk, Do it

things", I felt stressed and didn't come up with anything. As so often, you produce different results by changing the way you are looking at it.

I re-defined the word big for myself:

- Big for me was to do something physically challenging that I had not done before

You don't have to impress others: you can climb the Himalaya because this is what some people consider as big – but what if climbing is not your thing? You would not enjoy it and why should people follow an unhappy face? I chose something that I liked and that would make a "big" difference to me: Cycling around Spain. Even if the "branding" – or making money bit - would not work out, I still would have a physical endurance, some new language skills and fresh insights into a culture that I had barely visited before.

Don't just talk, Do it

Big is what you make it, not what you think it is.

Next destination: Accepting your emotional beasts

I picked, I got started and created momentum - ready to move forwards and making a great adventure happen, but there is one thing you unleash once you step out of your comfort zone: it's the emotional beast manifesting itself in form of doubts and worries. It creeps up on you, grabs your legs, slowing down your pace to take an action step and numbing your brain for decision-making, preventing you to come up with ideas and solutions.

But good news: it can be tamed. How? First, let's

Don't just talk, Do it

check out what it looks like in the "normal" world.

Welcome worry-cycle

These are some sentences that may sound familiar to you when setting the goal to accomplish a new project:

- The idea looks too big

- Everything seems too hard to be tackled

- You are overwhelmed and don't know where to start

- You think it's going to take forever until anything is going to change

- You want to hide in bed and put the idea back into **"idea / dream drawer"** – and think about it later

Once you have unleashed the beast, or the worry-

Don't just talk, Do it

cycle, I know it is pretty hard to get yourself motivated and easily tempted to put the dream on "hold". But stop right here, and do one thing: breathe and calm down.

If you cannot calm down, try these (they worked for me)

- Go outside, close to a street and look at a license plate of either a driving or a parked car. Only take a peek for a second, then look away and try to remember the digits. Then go to the next one

- Go for a jog – at least 30min and put on

Don't just talk, Do it

some of your favourite music

- Slowly count down from 10, and with every number concentrate on what you can hear, see and feel, then count further. Example: 10, I can hear a bird, see a tree and feel the inside of my woollen glove, 9 …

Calm down: Doubts and worries are normal

You are confronted by all kinds of feelings and thoughts everyday – even every minute. It's normal and when challenged by something new, they sometimes get much stronger and noisier.

Your brain uses old thinking patterns and memories, picking up on examples of the past, most likely negative ones, to find reasons of why it is not going to work out whatever you are trying to

Don't just talk, Do it

accomplish.

There is one quote that I use to remind myself when I am in this situation:

"Feelings only lie"

-Hale Dwoskin, author and teacher of

"The Sedona Method"

There is no stop-button or magic spell to make them go away – at least not straight away, but there are some good tools you can start using right now:

- **Number one:** realise that the thoughts you are trying to argue with are not real, but stories of the past

- **Number two:** let them be and take the action that has triggered them anyway

Start to welcome your doubts and worries (like a

Don't just talk, Do it

family member you don't like, but who appears at some parties anyway). Instead of fighting them – hit the ignore button and wait for the reality check. Do it anyway and let action speak – allow your mindset to be reset of what is possible and adjust your limits. At one point the complaining family member will leave the party and so will the nagging thoughts and suppressing feelings that are holding you back: they will loose their voice once you see that the result looks different. And when this happens, you are empowered by the belief that dreams are not just random ideas, but are there for a reason -and meant to be made come true. Here another quote from **Hale Dwoskin**:

"The only reason we want to understand our problems is because we are planning to have them again."

My intruders

Before I tell you an emotional story, here a

Don't just talk, Do it

reminder:

What was Mission Spain again?

It is the name of the cycle trip around Spain that I organised in 30 days including sponsorship and a wicked looking online-platform.

Less then a month of organisation, followed by two months of pure adventure.

Go here for more (**www.nadinehorn.com** -> Adventure -> Big)

Once I started with Mission Spain on the 1st of April, the challenge was not only to bring about the project, but also to challenge my old believes, ones

Don't just talk, Do it

I was not even aware of then. Here they come:

- I cannot make something happen that quickly

- The mission is too small for anyone to be interested

- I tried many times in the past, why should it work now (and many more)

Browsing through pages of big-time explorers like Bear Grylls and Ben Fogle to find inspiration, I only started doubting my "little" trip – overwhelmed by what the "real adventurers" had achieved. I just wanted to stop (and may be eat chocolate for comfort). My brain got tied-up and everything seemed to be a "ridiculous" idea.

I could have resigned, spending the following months on the question **"why I think this way"**, or as I did, ask myself the favour to just give it a try –

Don't just talk, Do it

ignoring the daunting feelings at least for 30 days.

So I followed the motto:

- Do the best you can, take one step at the time and let evidence be the guiding factor of what is possible

I grabbed my whiteboard and tuned myself into the **"doing mode"**, chunking down the overwhelming looking venture.

Ready for take-off: Chunk down the big picture

I was sitting on the floor of my room in Victoria Park, staring at my whiteboard – the only thing looking back at me was my project outline: Get paid to be an adventurer (or get branded as one). In 30 days this idea was supposed to have substance. How the hell is that going to happen? What are the steps I have to take? And most of all, what does

Don't just talk, Do it

this sentence actually mean in tangible terms?

―――――――――――――――――――――
―――――

Sometimes we use words and don't even know the meaning – hello, confusion!

―――――――――――――――――――――
―――――

Never had I done anything like this before, hence I had no idea where to start and which parts belonged to it – and what it meant to "brand" yourself. Questions were quickly multiplying in my head like bacteria (dividing themselves in a second – out of one you make two). I realized that I had no time to deal with them, if I wanted to see at least some result within my short deadline.

Don't spend too much time on finding

Don't just talk, Do it

answers, try out a different approach

To start doing "something", instead of figuring out of how to get to the final end product, I checked out whether I could break down the rough draft into smaller bits – and indeed I could:

- Adventure

- Branding (the marketing bit)

I began focusing on one part at a time. In order to get branded as adventurer, I needed one trip to start off with in the first place:

- With the re-definition of "big", choosing something that I would enjoy,

- And also making it useful to others (an addition from my 30 day challenge support community)

Don't just talk, Do it

What would I enjoy?

Here my weekend trips came in handy - they allowed me to explore what I was looking for in having a good-time with a learning curve: cycling trip over a longer period, having a purpose and destination plus learning a new language (inspired by the polish chap I met through couchsurfing).

This approach allowed me to choose my adventure and Mission Spain was born: Cycling around Spain. The worst case scenario of not fulfilling the second part of my project outline – to get branded – was to have spent some fun-time in Spain, returning home with some new language skills and some sportive outlet – more then acceptable (don't you think?).

What would be useful to others?

I thought that it could be quiet entertaining for people - even useful – to follow my travels by watching videos and reading blog posts. So, I

Don't just talk, Do it

decided to put up a blog that would document my trip.

———————————————————
——————

It's easier for other people to follow you, if you include them into your project – think about them and have something to share at the end of your deadline, or even steps along the way.

———————————————————
——————

Now the cloud in the sky had substance, from **"branding myself as adventurer"** I went to **"cycle around Spain, learning Spanish on the way and documenting my trip on a blog to share it with others"**.

Can you see what difference it makes, once you get started and change your approach? The picture

Don't just talk, Do it

becomes clearer and you naturally know what to do next.

Set yourself a deadline

"My goal is to hit the road at the start of May and then to be on the way for two months, coming back on time for a talk of Sir Richard Branson and Tony Robbins on the 2nd of July in London." **-post entry from Mission Spain**

Don't just talk, Do it

The cloud, even with some substance, can still keep floating up in the air if you are not committing yourself to a deadline. What difference does it make to have one? Giving yourself a target date increases the power of decision making: running out of time you realise that your ideal template of your to-do list has to make way for shortcuts. You have to act and have no time for too many questions and guessing – you play it out.

In the end those alternative routes are getting you there as well and sometimes even produce better results. A side effect of this is that you slowly change your perspective of how things can be done – hence expand you thinking pattern with possible ways to accomplish your mission.

My first deadline was to sign up for a 30 day challenge: it is easier to put your "worries" on hold for this time and change the way you do things (after that you can still go back to your **"old ways"**,

Don't just talk, Do it

but believe me you won't).

The next deadline was casual: I booked a ticket for a show in London that I wanted to see – so I had two months in between I could do the trip.

Did I know that it would be realistic to cycle around Spain in two months? (Big laughter) – hell no, when I made the decision I did not even had a look at a map of Spain, let alone an idea of a possible route – it was a random pick. Sense or no sense: you choose just like that and polish the edges as you go along.

There is a metaphor that I like to use when I am chunking something down:

— —
— — — — —

It is like building a house, you have this big picture and instead of not starting or starting everywhere

Don't just talk, Do it

you set the frame, the foundation and the rest kind of becomes clear as you go along.

Don't just talk, Do it

Don't just talk, Do it

Let your project evolve naturally

"You have to allow your project to evolve and take on a different shape."

-Selina Baker, Coach of 30 Day Challenge from

"Screw Work Let's Play"

We are control-freaks: We like to know how to get to the next stage - we want to be the ones making decisions, even over the outcome of the next step (as if we could possibly do this). We think that only if we suffer and work hard, can we make it. We want to push and push (did I mention control freaks) – even if it is in the wrong direction. Why do we do this: because we want to be in control, we want to know what the future brings and we want security. Does it sound familiar to you? Welcome on board.

Don't just talk, Do it

So what's that word about **"letting your project evolve naturally"**? It's about forgetting what you desire initially and be open to the direction your project is heading – trusting your gut-feeling with every step along the way. You will become more honest with yourself as you do what you enjoy (rather than following someone else's dream).

In my case it was about leaving behind the idea of what a successful adventure would look like.

Make a list and then forget about it

Already my outline had turned from "branding myself as adventurer" to "cycling around Spain, learning Spanish on the way and documenting the trip to share it with others" – now it was time for action, time to tackle the different elements - it was time to make a list.

I grabbed my whiteboard (let's call it Eddy here for the fun of it) and wrote down everything that sprang

Don't just talk, Do it

to my mind within 5 minutes:

To Do

- Everything required to kick-off the adventure

Need

- Bike

- Rucksack (can buy or borrow from a friend)

Things to Finish Before I Go

- Open jobs (finishing the article for the online magazine)

- Go to the doctor and get the usual check-up

You see the "list" was not full – not representing the whole **"how-to"**, it was only a mirror of what I knew at this point. I did not push it to make it larger or "work-out" all the "how-to's". I went for the natural evolution and accepted that this was what mattered for now. And it only took me 5 minutes: no effort, just fun and hence started creating momentum instead of pushing and setting ground for the potential **"avoiding reflex"** and **"procrastination"**.

It was my first list - my first rough cut and I trusted that it would fill itself once I got going – the next step was to look at one specific element and forget about the rest - forget about the list and put the whiteboard, Eddy, into the corner – one step at the time.

Pause: A word about "Brainstorming"

To be honest I never understood the term when I came across it – I was actually resisting it and feeling the urge to just skip the page when reading it in a "helping how to study effectively" book (it worked for others, but not for me). The idea of having to draw these ridiculous brainstorm diagrams (you know the ones with one big bubble in the middle and branches sticking out of it), was

Don't just talk, Do it

far away of what felt naturally to me – being given all these rules and seemingly necessary structures to be effective. After my last project however, I redefined the word for myself:

Brainstorming

Take 5 minutes now and write everything on a piece of paper that springs to your mind. Keep adding points, ideas or insights during the week while working on your project. At the end of the week take a new piece of paper and see whether you can give your list a structure with some headers. Keep adding ideas to this one.

While you are doing this exercise, keep it effortless

Don't just talk, Do it

and stop judging what comes up: at this point nothing is good or bad and even if it doesn't seem to make sense at all – write it down.

Here we go, the magic tool to speed things up: Step-by- Step

"...I feel really energized and it is a feeling that pushes away any question of how I am going to make things happen. I mean really just do one thing at the time. Let the next step come naturally as a result of the first one. You cannot see what is around the corner yet. And the last couple of days have showed me that amazing things can happen you could not have imagined." -**post entry from Mission Spain**

Don't just talk, Do it

When I first started off, I felt overwhelmed, freaked and had the **"no idea of how I am going to do this"** look on my face (like a reindeer staring into the head lights of a car). However, ticking off one thing after the other from my non-structured brainstorm list – it took me only 5 days until I shifted from having the **"reindeer look"** to being excited, growing confidence that by the end of my 30 day deadline, I would be ready to head-off. I was curious of what shape the project would take by tomorrow, but could not even think beyond the next step – the journey was just **"goose-bumps-ly"** awesome and mind blowing.

Branded Adventure

↓

Cycling around Spain learning Spanish on the way (addition after deciding on what I enjoyed)

Don't just talk, Do it

↓

Nadine's Bicycle Courier: she brings something from the village she leaves to the next one (idea of my Swedish friend Urban)

 # Simple motto with two mind-blowing side-products

The motto: baby steps – one at the time (picture a baby right now to tune yourself in). You make a brainstorm list to get an idea of possible things to do. But you don't plan the order, like from top to bottom. You start by taking any from the list, spent some time on it and then see what it reveals – what outcome it brings. You will realise that after one step other items from your list are not necessary any more. You will instinctively know which one to go after next.

By following this procedure, you will gain two amazing side-products (that are going to speed up

Don't just talk, Do it

your project even more):

- Creating energising momentum

- Natural evolution of the project

I was blown away by observing the outcome: first of all it was more fun doing it (no rules that would trigger the **"resisting-button"**) and secondly it was just striking to watch the project molding itself, revealing some new additions after every single step. I was not interested in the final result of the project anymore – the end of my daily discoveries - but what insight or tool – such as creating your own video – I would learn the next day. Here the best examples of how things evolved:

- Turning a simple-looking blog into a something more resembling a professional website. Discovering the meaning of the blog-terminologies: widgets, pages and links – and using them

Don't just talk, Do it

- Writing letters to sponsors I came across from one moment to the other and receiving a "yes" within a day

- Buying a flip-cam (an easy-to-handle video camera) and entering a whole new world of editing and sharing my own home-made videos

The above all happened effortless by being curious of what would come next and just "doing" it.

Making a list of your **"have to do's"**, creating neat looking lists that plan out the whole time-line, just produces stress (and we all hate this word): it all becomes planned, rigid and restricted – it becomes work and you forget why you are doing this in the first place. Plus, it takes away the natural flow, preventing your project to take the shape it deserves.

"Problems cannot be solved at the same level of

Don't just talk, Do it

awareness that created them."

-Albert Einstein

Introduction to micro blocks

Does the following sentence sound familiar to you:

- Tomorrow, I will take off the whole day to work on xy and z

No clue how many times I told myself this one, but in the end of the day I mostly had the same results: not being productive at all. I asked myself why and found an answer:

The more time you have, the more time you waste.

Don't just talk, Do it

Through John and Selina (leaders of the 30 day challenge I signed up for), I heard the first time about **"micro-blocks"**. They are defined as:

- A block of 5 to 30 minutes you set aside and decide on one thing you can do that produces leverage for your project in this timeframe

Adjusting them to fit my own nature, here my definition:

- A block of 20 minutes where I would tick-off one thing with the trick to keep breaking down the step until I could produce a visible result within this time.

Following this, I created momentum, getting closer to the final outline as with every step I took, I

Don't just talk, Do it

produced something (and it's in human nature that we feel proud and motivated once we accomplish something) – it was like having an intrinsic **"reward-mechanism"**, leading to the "want" of more.

To make sure that whatever I did next, made a difference to my project I asked myself the following question (again thanks to John and Selina):

> *"What simple thing has the most impact on my project in the least amount of time spent?"*
>
> **-John Williams and Selina Baker 2011**
>
> **screwworkletsplay.com**

With using this approach, imagine what you can produce in an hour, in two – or even in 30 days (I am smiling here). It also helps you with the following:

Don't just talk, Do it

- Sit down and get started

- Focus

Your can easily convince yourself to sit down for 20 minutes in comparison to **"spending a whole day on something"**. And as soon you do so and get into the productive vibe – hey – feel free to do overtime. Only be aware when you start to leave the productive stage and getting into the **"asking too many questions"** one. Then it's time to schedule the next block with impact. You will also be amazed of what ideas and approaches you come up with once you are totally immersed in one particular thing – why does it work for 20 minutes and not the whole day? The answer is simple: your brain has no "time" to get side tracked, its mission is to produce an outcome at the end of your block. In comparison a whole day has plenty of slots for idleness and questions.

These little brainchildren help you to become more

Don't just talk, Do it

productive with your time: allowing yourself to create space in between the blocks to re-asses your direction and letting go of figuring things out. If you really cannot accomplish a result in your set time-block, the step is too big and it needs to be broken down further. Making use of these helpers, you create a positive habit that speeds things up and make you enjoy whatever crazy idea you like to make happen. Everything becomes easier and more natural.

Another handy tip from John and Selina

- Make your block an appointment with yourself: give it the importance it deserves, switch off your emails, phone and lock the door – turning of any external distractions

----

Don't just talk, Do it

Mission Spain was born out of micro-blocks: I sat down, would take out a post-it note (next to my whiteboard "Eddy", another favourite helper), asked myself the question **"What simple thing has the most impact in the least amount of time spent"** and would break down the step at hand to fit it into the next 20 minutes with the goal to produce some outcome. I put the thought aside whether the point at hand was right or wrong – knowing that after 20 minutes I could adjust the direction if it turned out to go completely wrong. It all worked out.

Don't just talk, Do it

Don't just talk, Do it

Ask for help

In the past I was a lonesome-ranger, doing everything by myself and keeping my projects secret until they were visible: I followed the – I can do it myself / I don't need help – attitude.

Nothing wrong with that, only that sometimes you are missing out of two useful elements:

- Get somewhere faster

- Grow an idea bigger than you could have pictured in your wildest dreams

It's true that "you" or "I" can do things without anyone: eventually we will make it without "someone helping us" – proving ourselves of being strong and whatever other complex we try to compensate (we all have some). But if we are smart and like to make things easier and have more fun, we ask for help – making use of the

Don't just talk, Do it

knowledge and expertise that is already out there. It allows us to think about the essence of our project and delegate the sometimes un-enjoyable and time consuming practical layers to others (and guess what – for them it can be a new fun challenge to have fun with).

To get rid off any bad taste in your mouth when using the words "getting help" – let's redefine them here:

It means being clever and delegating areas of your undertaking to the experts.

Don't try so hard making it work by yourself, spending time learning things you don't like, and

Don't just talk, Do it

only doing it for the sake of getting the **"intelligent-stamp"** on your forehead: for once and all throw the phrase **"I need to work hard to succeed"** into the bin – now. Start trusting yourself that you could do everything if necessary, but at this moment enjoy playing around with more fun-stuff while others are happy to take over the rest.

The melting pot of talents

Here is what I call a melting pot of talents: there are your direct friends, the friends of your friends or the crowd you've once met and jotted down their email addresses in a little notebook. They are the people from all walks of life with all kinds of abilities, talents and experiences.

Next time you are stuck, haven't got the **"know-how"** or lacking experience to choose the best available option, ask one of them for help: send out an email to a person that is a "geek" in this field. In return, offer them something nice: invite them to a yummy dinner or a relaxing beer-catch up.

Banner Logo: My scream for help and the difference it made

Remember my intention of creating a stunning looking blog? A blog that looked like a website, an online-business card representing my project, telling others what I am all about: helping me to impress sponsors? So far I worked around the layout template (also called theme) and added text – very boring. I was missing three ingredients at this point:

- Colour

- Images

- Spice

The stunning-ness, the wow-factor once you opened the page was missing – the answer you

Don't just talk, Do it

can receive in 3 seconds to the question "what is this site about". I needed to swap the blog default banner (big picture at the top of the site) to something that outlined my whole project.

Sitting at my office desk, I tried to make this vision of the 3-sec-wow-banner happen.

My tools:

- The software paint (yeah, I mean the simple cut and paste drawing software that kiddies use on their dads computer)

- Internet access

I tried to use it for my best, copying and pasting some images (taken from the library of shutterstock.com) and fooling around. Here what the result looked like (yes, you can laugh):

Don't just talk, Do it

Mission Spain

Impressed? Me neither. As you can see, I had no idea, no tools and remember the deadline – no time. But I had one thing: friends in the graphic design area.

And they had three things:

- Knowledge
- Experience
- Tools

I grabbed the phone and called up my friend Johnny, approaching him with the following:

Don't just talk, Do it

"Hey Johnny, I am doing this project and have this problem of creating a stunning banner image for my site.

I only have this week to get it done, any chance you can help me out?"

I offered to help him with something else in return or invite him for dinner – he said yes and we met up the following weekend to produce the wow-factor version:

Don't just talk, Do it

Makes a difference or?

Three reasons why you are not asking for help

I was in need of some advice, I asked for it and I got it – not only for the banner logo, but for different parts along the way that altogether turned my idea into something exceptionally real in a very short-time. If you are having any problems - on whatever you are working right now – why are you not getting help? May be because of the following reasons? Let's have a look and de-mystify them.

Number 1:

You think that asking your buddies for help means

Don't just talk, Do it

"using" them (bad-mouth-taste-alarm!).

I don't know where this belief is coming from, but it is total bullsh***, you can ask anyone and everyone if they can lend you a hand – this has nothing to do with **"using"** or **"abusing"**. Plus, guess what? Yes, your friends are adults and as you have the permission to ask, they also have the permission to make their own decisions. Don't take this away from them, brave up and ask.

Number 2:

You are afraid they say no.

Yep, they can do so – but is it the end of the world, the end of your project? Of course not, it's just the beginning for a new approach achieving the same outcome. Be creative and look for a compromise that works for both of you. Going back to my **"Banner-asking-Johnny-for-his-expertise"** example, here my possible options if his answer

Don't just talk, Do it

would have been a "no":

- Asking him for a one-hour tutorial introducing me to the basic tools of photoshop

- See if he wouldn't mind to lend me his office space over the weekend using his computer

A "no" is never the end (you are not going to die of it), but gives ground for a new approach achieving the same or similar outcome.

Number 3:

You think that you don't know any "Johnny's" who can help you out that easily.

Well, that's possible, but then there are still two options you can choose from:

- Pay some non-related professional to do it

- Start building up a network of those friends

Don't just talk, Do it

that inspire you – or as I call it: start building up a team

Find yourself a good team

If you realise that for some reason you are not surrounded by people that inspire you: it's time to go out and find them, building up a network of individuals that understand you and are all about making ideas real. It's time you get yourself a team.

Before we get into the "how-to" lets talk about the difference between friends and a team.

First things first: Team vs. Friends

Believe me a team can be, but normally is not fixed for a life-time (and sometimes friends are). It's because your ideas change, your lifestyle does and with this yourself, including your visions and the challenges you like to conquer. It's a natural and normal flow and once it happens, the network of

Don't just talk, Do it

people who support and inspire you, changes as well - your team evolves.

So what are the main differences between a team and your friends?

- It does not doubt your plan, it helps you to fulfil it

- You don't go to them for complaints, but to find a solution

- The connection between you and your team is: Creation

A team is plainly that:

A body of knowledge, experience and expertise that is looking for solutions, instead of meeting up for a "shit" chat engraving your doubts. It gives you a hand to throw any disbelief of **"not possible"** into the bin and expand your view – helping you to create powerful thinking patterns.

Two ways to find you one

It's not so difficult to get started, there are two main things you can do right now to get yourself a team (or start growing it):

Number 1:

- *Become selective when looking for advice*

Next time you are stuck and decided to get help or delegate a task that's not in the field of your interest, hang on a second before you just dial "a number". Think of a person whose lifestyle or work you are inspired by? Who has the same approach to life than you do and can give you a good

Don't just talk, Do it

answer? Being selective means to bunch up people that:

- Have the knowledge

- Are as enthusiastic and passionate about life (or having a vision) as you are

Number 2:

- *Find yourself an inspiring hero with a matching community*

Changing your way of living and trying out something new often requires different tools - and most of the time, it comes when you join a community that has a different outlook. Here my example: My idea was to do adventures and make it my career. The question:

- Which job do I fit?

The answer: None. Trying to find the perfect job

Don't just talk, Do it

description, I got stuck. It's like baking a sweet cake and you only use salty ingredients – the combination will never work. When you get to this point, it's time to ditch the old recipe and create a new one. I had to build up my lifestyle on a different foundation, changing my perspective of how things work in society and gather new tools: I found the **"Scanner"** community:

A monthly event for creative people and entrepreneurs with multiple interests and lots of ideas (Scanners). The biggest challenge for them is how to make them happen quickly.
www.scannercentral.co.uk

Don't just talk, Do it

I was drawn to this particular bunch of people, because they tackled questions I was curious about. It changed my perspective from:

- Which job do I fit" to

- How can I create my own"

Look out for communities that are doing what you are interested in: turn up, listen and talk to the crowd, ask your questions. You don't have to agree with everything they say, but find some pieces that fit your puzzle - giving you inspiration of how to make your thing work.

One tip here: join a group that has a leader who has created results – some you like to manifest in your own life. It's good to follow someone who has proven that it works what he talks about (you don't want to waste your time).

 # Not only have a team, but become a team

Don't just talk, Do it

player

Have you found yourself yet a bunch of compatible stimulating minds – people you can go to for inspiration and advice? Yes? Well done.

Here two tips from experience that helped me to make good use of our times when working together.

Number 1:

- *Get to know the nature of the person*

To explain this one, here an example: In the final stage of my Mission Spain project I wanted to create a 3 minute trailer (like the ones you know from the movies) of my collected video material. I called up a friend who is a geek in this field to see if he could help me to make this happen. He was very busy, finishing off some university assignments, so he said no. I respected that but double checked on a compromise:

Don't just talk, Do it

- If he can show me in an hour how to create 3 things with the editing program

One hour was acceptable for both of us. For me it meant cutting down the time finding tutorials and spending it on working out the basics – for him it was an hour break from his studies. We met up and were ready to rumble. But, instead of explaining me my **"3 things"** he began to share "all" his knowledge about the program - for him as an expert it all mattered: it's his nature to do things in this way. However, for me it would not have been productive as most properly by the end of his precious hour, I still would not know how to tackle my 3 editing problems.

So:

- Get to know how your team-member ticks and find a way to be productive with both of your times (if time is an issue). Know what you want to have by the end of your catch-

Don't just talk, Do it

up

In my case I reminded him of the main problems at hand we agreed before and the scarcity of his time - appreciating his knowledge about this area. He understood and it worked.

Number 2:

- *Respect the flow of your team-member*

If you are not short on time and your expert isn't either, be open to what he can incorporate into your project. The reason you are sitting next to him is because you were lacking the idea of "how-to" or an inspiration that would make a difference. Don't resist something because you cannot see it yet, but wait until he has played it out. He has time and experience – use it.

Don't just talk, Do it

Don't just talk, Do it

Dare to share – emotions, doubts and hey, your actual project

Old dusty thinking patterns are not only the reasons why we don't seek help, but also hold us back to share. We keep things to ourselves: our emotions, doubts and ideas – and at the same time miss out on learning, solving and providing leverage to what we believe in.

Why do we do that? Maybe for these reasons:

- We think we need to appear strong

- We also assume that we are not allowed to have doubts, because if we do, we think we have failed

- We don't want to show off

- Whatever we are doing is not good enough

Don't just talk, Do it

I don't know where all those paralysing thoughts are coming from: everyone has them once in a-while but some learn to throw them out, ignore them when they pass by in our brains and remind themselves of the following:

What's happening if we don't share?

We don't know if certain emotions that come up with the next action step are real: if they make sense – if we don't share them, we take away the reality check. If we are not open / afraid for whatever reason to keep our project to ourselves, we miss out of making it grow bigger and sometimes actually doing it. Plus, your idea has the right to be shared.

Don't just talk, Do it

Go and tell someone now about what you are doing or want to do. The time for keeping it secret is over (only to your benefit).

What if my idea gets stolen?

Do you think if you share your idea it will get stolen? Totally normal – I did: I was first reluctant to put any news and updates of **"Mission Spain"** on the blog - out of fear someone would pinch it and with this my sponsors and followers. A wise person, however, reminded me of the following:

- If you are in the project, no one can steal your idea, as they miss the vision and passion you bring on the table. Hence the reason, why yours is going to be unique no matter what.

So forget about the **"I cannot share it because someone will steal it"** – just go out and do it. Only be careful if you sell a fresh product, not involving

Don't just talk, Do it

you as a person – make sure you have a patent or a copyright before sharing it with the world (to be on the save side).

Sharing vs. Complaining

Two words, totally different in meaning and the outcome it creates, but still mixed up at times. Sometimes people go to their friends with the intention to share, but the only thing they do without noticing is that they complain: they tell a story of what is wrong and go over it again and again. They could ask their buddies, what's faulty and seek advice, but instead hang-on to the bad situation – and the story. Secretly, perhaps on the sub-conscious level, they enjoy being the victim and hence continue to complain.

Don't just talk, Do it

So here the "One Million Dollar Question":

Would you stop doing something you enjoy?

(Congratulations, you just won)

What's sharing then? It's the process of making people part of your journey: not only telling the worries and the doubts, but all the good stuff and excitement it reveals. The **"problem stories"** are only told once or twice, because your share them to find a solution. If you realise that you are repeating yourself on several occasions about the same issue – it's time to deal with it differently.

Don't just talk, Do it

Why sharing is so essential: Example Mission Spain

My learning curve was ignited by Mission Spain: in order to make use of my talented team, I had the obligation to share – the good and the bad things. How can someone help you to overcome an obstacle or provide some juicy addition to your project, if they don't know what you are up to? You simply have to share, when working in a team.

Example: When "fear" bubbled up inside of me, I questioned my team to get perspective on it: is the feeling justified, or not?

Another benefit for me of spreading the word, was to become clear on the project itself. When writing the letters to the sponsors, it was essential to know what I was doing, what my intention was and the benefit it would bring to others.

Don't just talk, Do it

——————————————————
—————

Sharing helps you to adjust your idea – so that it works – and allows it to grow bigger, using the input others give you.

——————————————————
—————

Turning a "blog" into your "site"

You can make your project public in many ways, using some really good fun tools such as writing a blog, producing videos or making audio recordings.

When it was time for me too choose a medium, I went for a blog: creating a platform similar to an

Don't just talk, Do it

online business card representing my project.

A word about blogs

Blog: a word that has become very trendy with all kinds of clichés attached to it, such as the one I found on *thebadblogger.com*:

- Writing with having nothing to say

I am not a **"blogger"**, but simply someone using the tool of having access to a free online landing site – one that allows me to attract people to a particular happening.

Hence I prefer to say: "Check out my site" instead of "check out my blog" – preventing to trigger any "wrong" ideas. It's like saying "I am German" and people ask the question "So you like sausage".

Free is good, but can hide a little danger: I have previously set up 7 blogs to play around with. Yes, 7. Whenever I had an idea, I created a blog – soon

Don't just talk, Do it

the passion over the initial undertaking died and with it the page. Now you can imagine that I was a bit resistant to set up yet another blog for a mission that I intended to succeed.

I had to make myself a promise: to create a professional website-looking site and not just a free blog. Now you may ask: Why did I not set up a website? Did I mention that it's free, easy to build, maintain and change? Did I mention time – 30days? So it seemed the obvious at this point – how I made use of it to create a site rather than a blog? Keep reading.

First: Wordpress vs. Blogger

These two are blog providers. I chose *Wordpress* over *Blogger*, because starting a Google search, using the combination: Wordpress and **"how-to tutorials"** simply yielded more results. It is good to have support, when getting stuck. Another plus point for Wordpress was that you can buy a ".com" domain and convert your blog into a proper website.

The perfect name does not exist

I set up "my site" (remember I don't like the word "blog") right at the beginning of my 30 days challenge with the intention to document the journey and use it as approach for sponsors. By then I had not clue where the project was heading or what it was yet to become, so imagine the thoughts and fear sneaking in:

- Whatever name I choose, it is not going to be the right one

- Once I choose one, there is no turning back

- If the name is wrong, my project is pruned to fail

That was not helping, too much pressure and tension for the brain. Again, my deadline was tight:

Don't just talk, Do it

no time for thinking "perfect" and I told myself that I am going to use a name that is representing my project at this time, that I can always change it and will find a way to keep the readership once I do so – I accepted that it is only a name and not the project itself. I took my pick:

- cyclearoundspain.wordpress.com

The point is that you have to choose with the knowledge you have right now – the perfect time is never there – you trust yourself that when the moment has come and you have more enlightenment, you are open for changes and trust yourself that you will work it out (never get too attached to one particular part of your project).

Getting into the habit of "choosing" instead of "wondering" about "perfect", teaches you to do, trust and change when the time has come.

Same goes for the theme (blogger terminology for: layout)

Same for the style: you can spent a lot of time trying to find the most stunning layout or pick one that does the job for now, being open for changes and making adjustments as you go along. I first played around with all the templates Wordpress had to offer – not one gave me the **"final picture"**, the final site I had in mind, but again I had no time for anger and frustration and just picked one. It turned out that with time, help and the following tools, the layout evolved into what I was looking for:

- Inserting own pictures

- Creating banners

Don't just talk, Do it

- Adjusting side-bars
- Pages
- Static sites
- Slideshows and galleries
- Widgets

What I learned: Again don't waste too much time to get everything supreme at the start - some things need time to develop. The whole process of setting up the site was a learning curve with the following insights.

Start to play around – let go of what you want

We make up our minds of what we want – but at the same time have no plan in what an idea can grow into. The same accounts for your site / blog.

Don't just talk, Do it

I wanted to have a final online-business card that looked stunning and would give the project leverage. I had no vision of the exact elements that would make it look-like that – so at this point impatience, frustration and hence paralysis popped-up:

- How do I turn this thing into something that is going impress sponsors?

It was time to let go of what I wanted, but to have fun, taking one step at the time instead of wanting to make it happen all at once.

Remember this? Step-by-step

So before doing nothing, when you feel the picture is too big and you freak out, its time for baby-steps.

I was getting frustrated with the site that was essential to get equipment support, so I started to approach it in a different way, looking for answers

Don't just talk, Do it

to the following:

What do I not like about it?

- **Answer:** that it looks like a blog – I don't want to approach sponsors with "hey this is my blog", but to have something more powerful to present – a website.

- **Step:** Find out what is the difference between a blog and a site regarding layout.

- **Answer:** A website has an entry page (also called static page), a menu with different pages.

- **Question:** Can I create something similar with my Wordpress blog?

- **Answer:** yes.

I didn't allow anything to make me stuck: if I had a question and could not work it out in 2 minutes I looked for a key word and put it into Google – if the first three entries did not come up with any good answers, I changed the keyword becoming more selective or looked for someone who could help me with this: I was focused and selective – all enhanced by my 30 day deadline.

Get answers, don't look for more questions: The problem with forums and full-text sites

Be aware of forums when you look for answers: in a forum people now and then just complain and start discussing for ages. But in the end don't come up with any good answers to their questions (a lot of talking, no results). If they, however, have a solution – it is buried somewhere in the whole conversation – not that easy for you to find (like the needle in the haystack).

The same goes for sites that are full of text – you

Don't just talk, Do it

need to filter out the right steps yourself to solve a problem. It only takes your precious time and can lead to frustration (and we don't want that – do we?). Instead, give yourself a happy face and a productive time by only using sites that show you in a step-by-step guide manner how to crack an issue. You want to know the "how" and not agree with people having the same problem, or spend ages reading a text.

One of my team members introduced me to the perfect support page for my Wordpress problems:

- http://en.support.wordpress.com

When hitting a **"don't know"** obstacle, I straight went to this page and typed in the topic. After a minute or two, I had a result, listing the steps to create what I was looking for.

Don't just talk, Do it

Let's to a test to show you what I mean:

- Type into Google the word combination: static, blog, layout

- Check out the first couple of pages and see if you find an answer

- Now go to the link I mentioned before and type the word "static" into the search field

- Check out the first entries

- See the difference?

This test was not about forums, but to clarify what

Don't just talk, Do it

the difference it makes to have a 1,2,3 guide presenting "how" to reach your aim, instead of the need to keep scrolling through a text to find them.

Once you have a reliable source, go straight to it when having a question. Don't waste too much time on the internet: it is honestly not worth it. If your source does not come with anything, grab the phone and call someone for help. Save yourself time.

Don't just talk, Do it

Don't just talk, Do it

Money is not the limiting factor to get you started

Now you are ready, you have:

- Taken your pick

- Chunked down your dream into approachable baby-steps

- Surrounded yourself with a great team and

- Have put your emotional beasts on a leash

Now we come to one factor that plays a big role for many: money. It's already in the header, but let me repeat it to ingrain it into your innermost self:

―――――――――――――――――――――――――――

Don't let money decide whether you are ready for

Don't just talk, Do it

something crazy – the time is never right

How do I dare say this you might ask? Guess what, I speak from experience: one idea, one month to prepare the whole thing and in the end it all worked out, flying off to Spain to start my adventure. From the cap taking me to the airport, over a language-course and equipment to the bike itself – everything was covered (and believe me, my bank account wasn't stashed with cash). So, what did I do? I tried the creative approach and it worked. Money is good to have, but not the decision maker if something is possible.

We think that wealth rules the world, fixes problems and we need it to get started – I disagree. You work

Don't just talk, Do it

with what you have got and become creative.

Secret revealed: The two things that made it happen

Here they are:

- Sponsors

- Spread the word, using something you have to offer

Sponsors

I did not have sufficient savings (or monthly income) to sort myself out with equipment under the given deadline. Hence, the idea of sponsors popped into my head. Before Mission Spain, the word **"Sponsors"** sounded like a big word with no personal connection. Did I ever dream of someone supporting one of my undertakings earlier? Not in my wildest. But, once committed to accomplish my undertaking, I thought **"why not"**: and at this very moment **"writing letters to sponsors"** was added to my whiteboard to-do list.

I had no idea where to start, what to write or what to provide in return: more questions and doubts than answers.

Your project is not too small

Besides all the practical questions of:

- Where to find them?

- Who would be interested in supporting me?

- What would they sponsor?

- What would I write them?

Don't just talk, Do it

There was one overwhelming fear that first held me back from going out and doing it straight away:

- My idea is too small

I imagined that only first class adventurers are worth receiving some kind of sponsorship. It took me a day to swallow this belief (after my team kicked my ass) and to begin browsing the internet for inspiration to solve the practical questions. But, again coming across big time achievers, such as Sarah Outen – first and only woman rowing solo the Indian Ocean - fear bubbled up that my project was too small and ridiculous.

I just wanted to stop everything and welcomed another worry cycle:

- Why would someone even read my letters if I only cycle around Spain?

- My project is doomed

Don't just talk, Do it

- I will never get sponsors, I will never have enough financial support – I won't have a bike

- Long story, short: Mission Spain is not going to happen

I did not feel like a person that had permission to ask others to be interested in my project. So what did I do? I put the little internal struggle out to my inspirational team members and someone reminded me of the following: everyone has to start somewhere and when conquering new borders, it's normal that the fear is strong. So instead of allowing the "feeling" to kill my spirit, I set it aside (it was still there) with the intention to try it anyway and make the reality check. I asked myself the following:

- What is the worst thing that can happen if you do it anyway?

Don't just talk, Do it

The answer: People say no, so what? Then I approach someone else, fine-tuning the style of my request.

Approach your heroes, you will be amazed

Accepting that I was going for it, I still had one problem: I had no idea where to start. For some reason we think that people who are doing big things are not approachable – wrong. Most of the times you can find an email on their site, the question is:

- Have you ever dared to write them?

I needed help – and where to find the best than to ask someone who has succeeded? I went back to the site of Sarah Outen and wrote her a short, precise sentence if she had any advice for me. 3 hours later I had a reply in my inbox.

A reply (screaming excitement): someone took the

Don't just talk, Do it

time to read my email and even wrote back. My initial fear of failing turned into pure exhilaration.

This is why it is important to go out and do things: you grow bigger within yourself and realise that whatever fear is popping up inside may not even have reasons to be there. You get goose-bumps once you connect to your heroes or other people that support what you are up to.

The email was written by one of her team members (Sarah herself was off to another expedition) and let me forget all my doubts, ready to take action. She wrote:

- **If you don't ask, you don't get, so give it a go**

A motto that became my own - she ended the letter with:

- I will be thinking of you and good luck

Don't just talk, Do it

I felt part of something bigger. I felt energised and it just showed me that you just have to reach out and do things. I was ready for the next step.

Writing the letter: What can you offer?

I made a list of the areas I required some back-up: the bike, a Spanish course and general equipment, like the tent and a rucksack. The intention was not to receive money, but support in a form that allowed me to start my venture.

With the three areas in mind I Googled for companies and came across: organisation for hiring bikes, agencies providing language courses and bike shops for the general purpose. I sat down, jotting down the outlines of an email.

The content:

- You tell them who you are
- What you do and have done (and no

Don't just talk, Do it

shyness here, I mentioned all the good companies I worked for)

- Why you are doing this

I wrote everything down that could allow them to draw picture of who I was – I even attached two pictures. But, most importantly I added one section:

- What is in for you?

Sponsors are part of a business – working together with them I assume it has to be a win-win situation. They want something in return for their support. What I could offer was publicity.

Having created a stunning site, I offered them:

- Their name on my front page with a link to their website

- A separate section with a bit of content

Don't just talk, Do it

In addition, I mentioned that I would spread the word in my film and journalism network along with approaching radio stations and Spanish newspapers to make the project known.

The last paragraph of my letter contained my beneficial part:

- How can you help me

I added a list of the main equipment that was missing and asked them to take their pick. It's good to be clear of what you want from them, but at the same time give some flexibility and allow them to choose.

Keep asking: spread the word – other cash corners

Once I sent off the first letter, it was easier to sit down and write more, approaching other companies. The result: receiving positive replies

Don't just talk, Do it

even the following day.

Next to the sponsors, I still wanted to back up myself, just in case. So with the same motto:

- If you don't ask you don't get,

I looked for ways to make some extra cash (beside my day job): I approached the local weekend market and checked if they were looking for more staff. They did. I also signed up with a tutorial agency, giving kids support with their homework. Every little bit helped me to make some extra money and it all made a difference.

If you think you need more cash, find out if your friends who have a business need some help. Check if you have some skills that you can offer to someone for something in return: cash, equipment or knowledge. Create direct or indirect "cash" corners helping you to earn or save money. Be creative.

Don't just talk, Do it

I even rented out my flat a bit earlier to save the monthly rent you put down in advanced. I saved.

The secret is to create more branches to receive: it takes off the pressure that other people / supporters have to say yes – it keeps it fun and playful. Don't rely on just one source.

Don't just talk, Do it

Don't just talk, Do it

Done and dusted, enjoy the outcome

You have committed your energy to one particular thing (congratulation, you have been brave and made a choice), conquered your emotional beasts, reached an immense level of personal growth and learned many things on your way – and you have dared and done it, ticked off one of your dreams. You could not have imagined at the start where it would lead you, but you let go of the **"how-to-get-there"** and allowed your project to take shape by itself, giving it permission to grow to its **"bigger self"**. You are amazed and impressed, you are there. So now, off to the next one? STOP!!!!

- Don't forget to enjoy.

Take the time to pat yourself on the shoulder – it takes courage to do what you believe in and once you have done it, you deserve to enjoy it. Sit down

Don't just talk, Do it

and let all the emotions of this realisation flow through you. Give your brain a time-out to accept that you have broken old limits and thinking-habits and defined a new reality for yourself of what is possible.

It is easy to keep going once you realise it's all possible but hey, refill your energy tanks and relax – life is not about ticking off all the boxes, but to enjoy it - a break is part of it. Give yourself a little holiday to relax and enjoy what is now because you have created the outcome: it did not happen by chance or because someone did it for you – you went out and took chances. Life is what you make it. What will you make of yours?

Don't just talk, Do it

About the author

Nadine is a creative adventurer, author, speaker, seminar leader, corporate trainer & entrepreneur.

Head over to www.nadinehorn.com to read all about her.

Join her on Facebook: Get moving - adventurously & follow her on Twitter @Adventure_Nads

What'ts next: Nadine loves feedback. If you have enjoyed the book & it has inspired you do things differently, then write a little endorsing review. The book is self-published, if you are a literary agent or publishing house get in touch to discuss the possibility of cooperation.

Don't just talk, Do it

Conclusion

The book is meant to give insight into a different approach: giving you useful tools to go out and do things. Everything mentioned in here, allowed me to get Mission Spain off the ground and I was amazed by the outcome. I hope it does the same for you.

Sometimes it is good to read parts of the book and then put it aside – trying out the different aspects yourself: remember doing does the difference to talking and just reading.

Don't just talk, Do it

Acknowledgments

It's all about teamwork – so a big thank you to everyone who has jumped on board helping me out to make this book happen.

Marcos Villalba, thank you to create this stunning book-cover and I promise that the job of designing the book cover goes to you once I am published properly.

Thanks Steve and Paolo for allowing me to "abuse" your printer and for your patience.

A big thank you to my "master" editor James Mc Cormack, for making me aware of my semi-colons and offering valuable alternatives – I miss you in the Stag Irish dude.

Thank you to Brigida Marovelli and Ula Lipinska for having one of the first read through and giving me good feedback. Hope it's a bit lighter and funnier

Don't just talk, Do it

now, Ula.

Gabe Grieve, you are a legend, for jumping on board last minute, spicing up my book with your awesome sketches. Enjoy Australia.

At this point another thank you to Australia – thanks Dave (or triathlon champ) for reading through my first two pages, reminding me which bits not to cancel.

Huge thank you to John Williams and Selina Barker (together with the 30 Day Challenge Community) for being one of my support teams to give kick-ass reminders, reminding me that my ideas are possible – the only question is **"How to make it happen"**.

Where would this book be without the adventure "Mission Spain" itself? It would not exist. So here huge thank you to all the people that have crossed my path on my undertaking - making me feel

Don't just talk, Do it

welcome and sharing their passion for Spain with me. Thank you to all the Couchsurfer who offered me a sofa to rest, looked-after me and gave me the opportunity to reenergise my batteries to complete my trip with success.

Thanks to Xavier Rodriguez from Vision Creator to give me some good video-inspiration. Thank you to the Wimbledon Film Club for equipment advice.

Muchas gracias Iker(ito) Ganuz(ito) (disculpa, me gusta el nombre) – por compartir tu familia en Barcelona y Pamplona conmigo. No puedo dar las gracias con palabras pero sí con el corazón a Jesús, Kamele y Ana en Pamplona – por hacerme sentir como una hija y hacérmelo pasar increíble. Viva San Fermin.

A big thank to my Sponsors on Mission Spain: Linguaschools, Bravo Bike, Zweirad Schmid.

Hopefully I have not forgotten anyone, but if I have

Don't just talk, Do it

and you read this: thanks to you as well.

Don't just talk, Do it

Summary

1. Just take your pick and get started

- Get moving, get unstuck
- Too many options = too many questions = limbo
- Change your decision as you go along

2. Dare to dream big, yep, believe it's possible

- What is big anyway?
- Next destination: Accepting your emotional beasts
- Calm down: Doubts and worries are normal
- Read for take-off: Chunk down the big

Don't just talk, Do it

picture

3. Let your project evolve naturally

- Make a list and then forget about it

- Here we go, the magical toll to speed things up: Step-by-Step

4. Ask for help

- The melting pot of talents

- Find yourself a good team

5. Dare to share: Emotions, doubts and hey, your actual project

- The melting pot of talents

- Find yourself a good team

Don't just talk, Do it

6. Money is not the limiting factor

- What if my idea gets stolen?

- Sharing vs. Complaining

- Why sharing is so essential: Example Mission Spain

- Turning a 'blog' into your 'site'

7. Done and dusted, enjoy the outcome

Don't just talk, Do it

Printed in Great Britain
by Amazon.co.uk, Ltd.,
Marston Gate.